Paper Flowers

by Malia Nabors
illustrated by Colin Chang

Practice Pre-Decodable 7

Mc Graw Hill Education

Bothell, WA • Chicago, IL • Columbus, OH • New York, NY

MHEonline.com

Send all inquiries to:
McGraw-Hill Education
8787 Orion Place
Columbus, OH 43240

ISBN: 978-0-02-140446-9
MHID: 0-02-140446-1

Printed in China.

9 10 11 12 13 DSS 27 26 25 24 23

The  children had  paper.

The  had .

children crayons

The  had .

children scissors

The  had 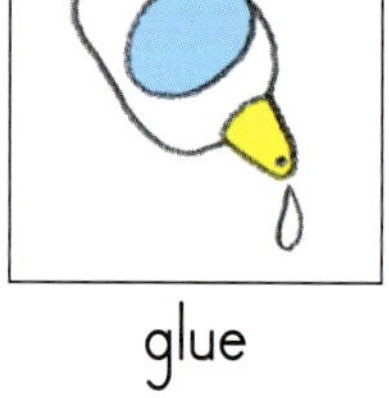.

children glue

The  had .

children flowers

The  had .

teacher flowers